Antarctic Life Who Lives There?

Curious Kids Press

Introduction

The Antarctica is the fifth largest continent in the world. This frosty region is covered by 98 percent ice, which can make living here very tough. The Antarctica is the windiest, coldest and driest of all the areas in the world. It is, in fact, considered a desert. Like hot deserts, this cold one does not get a lot of rain, either - about 8 inches (200 millimeters) each year. And that's around the coast. Read on to discover more cool facts and interesting creatures found in the Antarctic.

Weddell Seal

Did you know this species of seal lives on fast ice? This type of ice is attached to the shore or between two icebergs. The Weddell Seal can tolerate the icy waters of the Antarctic and will spend most of its time in the freezing waters. This seal will also chew holes in the ice to breathe through.

Leopard Seals

Did you know the Leopard Seal is the second largest seal on Earth? It can grow to be around 1,300 pounds (589 kilograms). Some measure around 11 feet long (3,3 meters). This Antarctic animal can be very aggressive. It likes to eat fish, krill and penguins.

Orcas

Did you know Orcas are also called, Killer Whales? These mammals will travel long distances (migrate) to find food and to have their young. Orcas can grow to be very large. They can measure up to 33 feet long (10 meters) and weigh in at more than 12,000 pounds (5.400 kilograms).

Blue Whales

Did you know this whale has 2 to 14 inches (5-30 centimeters) of thick blubber? This fat helps keep the whale warm in the cold water. The Blue Whale is the loudest mammal on Earth. It is louder than a jet engine. Its low frequency whistle can be heard for hundreds of miles.

Eastern Rockhopper Penguin

Did you know this species of penguin loves to hop around on the rocks? The Eastern Rockhopper Penguin can withstand the extreme climates of the Antarctic. In fact, this penguin has very few predators on land. The rockhopper also loves the chilly water and is a very good swimmer.

Chinstrap Penguin

Did you know there are around 14 million Chinstrap Penguins on the small Antarctic islands? These penguins are known for the black line of feathers under their chins. These penguins love the chill of the ocean waters and hunt for krill, shrimp, crabs and squid.

Black-browed Albatross

Did you know this Antarctic seabird can live to be over 70 years old? The Black-browed Albatross is a bird with a large wingspan. It can reach lengths of up to 94 inches (240 centimeters). This bird has black markings over its eyes that look like eyebrows.

Antarctic Shag

Did you know this bird dives under the chilly Antarctic waters to find its food? This bird sort of looks like a penguin, but it swims on top of the water like a duck. It has short legs and a long neck. This bird will feed on mostly crustaceans and fish..

Southern Elephant Seal

Did you know the Elephant Seal is the largest seal in the Antarctic? This big guy is easily recognized by his huge, bulbous nose. Males of this species can weigh up to 8,800 pounds (4,000 kilograms)! They are clumsy when on land, but are excellent divers. In fact, this elephant seal can hold its breath for 20 minutes.

Icefish

Did you know this cold water fish has no red blood cells? This makes it look quite odd. This fish lives deep in the cold Antarctic waters and does not need blood. Its body is filled with lots of oxygen. The Icefish can grow from 9.8 to 29 inches long (25 to 75 centimeters). It dines on krill, fish and crustaceans.

Colossal Squid

Did you know this squid is one of the largest? It can measure up to 46 feet long (14 meters). The Colossal Squid has very long limbs. Each one has suckers, teeth and sharp hooks on them. This cold-water creature also has very large eyes. Each one measure 11 inches across (27 centimeters).

Belgica Antarctica

Did you know the Belgica Antarctica is the only true insect found in this frigid region? This tiny flightless midge may be hard to spot. It only measures about 0.236 inches long (6 millimeters). This insect is very tough. It can come back from freezing and can go without oxygen for up to 4 weeks!

Antarctic Hair Grass

Did you know this plant is one of only a few types of plants that grow in the Antarctic? The Antarctic Hair Grass grows along the coastline. It has long dark green stems and it can grow along with moss among the rocks. This plant is not like the grass you see in a park. It is very strong and tough.

Antarctic Pearlwort

Did you know this is one of only two plants that has flowers in the Antarctic? The Antarctic Pearlwort looks sort of like moss. It only grows 2 inches tall (5 centimeters). It has small, pretty, white flowers in the warmer months. It grows around the rocks.

People in the Antarctic

Did you know there are no native people that live in the Antarctic? The only people who come to this cold region are researchers and tourists. There are no towns, restaurants, stores or industries in the Antarctic. It is just too cold and harsh for people to stay here for very long.

Quiz

Question 1: Which Antarctic seal is the second largest on Earth?

Answer 1: The Leopard Seal

Question 2: Which whale has super-thick blubber?

Answer 2: The Blue Whale

Question 3: Which Antarctic penguin has weird markings on its face?

Answer 3: The Chinstrap Penguin

Question 4: How can the Icefish survive in such cold water?

Answer 4: It does not have any red blood cells

Question 5: What is one of the only insects found in the Antarctic?

Answer 5: The Belgica Antarctica

Thank you for checking out another title from Curious Kids Press! Make sure to search "Curious Kids Press" on Amazon.com for many other great books.

CPSIA information can be obtained
at www.ICGtesting.com
Printed in the USA
LVHW070429191120
672140LV00001B/8

ISBN 9781499542967

90000

9 781499 542967